Miscellaneous Artwork as Capital Assets

By Rachel Soloveichik

Abstract

In 2007, I estimate that playwrights, artists, photographers and designers created miscellaneous artwork worth $3.3 billion. By category, theatrical play scripts were $1.4 billion, greeting card designs were $0.5 billion and commercial stock photography was $1.4 billion. Taken individually, each of the entertainment categories described earlier are too small to examine in a single paper. Therefore, I combine all three categories into a single paper.

These diverse categories of artwork will earn revenue for their creators for decades to come. Because of their long working life, the international guidelines for national accounts recommends that countries classify production of all entertainment originals as an investment activity and then depreciation those entertainment originals over time. However, BEA did not capitalize this category of intangible assets until the July 2013 benchmark revision. In order to change the national accounts, I collected data on miscellaneous artwork production back to 1900. I then calculated how the GDP statistics would change when miscellaneous artwork is classified as a capital asset.

To preview, my empirical results are:
 1) Miscellaneous artwork has grown slower than the overall entertainment industry. In 1929, miscellaneous artwork accounted for 9% of total entertainment investment. In 2007, miscellaneous artwork was only 5% of entertainment. Therefore, I would underestimate historical investment and overestimate growth rates if I ignored miscellaneous artwork;
 2) Miscellaneous artwork includes a heterogeneous group of products. Each individual category has different nominal growth rates, price indexes and depreciation schedules.

Introduction

This paper will consist of three sections. In section 1, I describe my data on performance art such as theatrical plays, opera, dance and other live artwork. In that section, I estimate nominal investment, prices and depreciation rates for scripts from 1929 to 2010. In section 2, I describe my data on greeting card design and report nominal investment, prices and depreciation rates from 1929 to 2010. In section 3, I describe my data on commercial stock photography and report nominal investment, prices and depreciation rates from 1929 to 2010.

I have also considered counting other entertainment categories like fine art reproduction and comic strip formats in the miscellaneous artwork group. However, I was not able to find reliable data on fine art reproductions back to 1929. Furthermore, the OECD's handbook on intellectual property (OECD 2010) does not mention format rights in the category entertainment originals. Accordingly, I will not include those categories in this paper.

1. Performance Art

In this paper, I only count play scripts, dance choreography, musical scores and other copyrightable works as long-lived capital assets. These script originals exist independently from a particular play run. For example, it is common for directors to license a classic play and adapt it to an all new cast. I do not count the implicit capital value of cast selection, rehearsal time and other preparation as a capital asset. Unlike play scripts works, these production costs are tied to the individual actors involved in a particular play run – and so they are a form of human capital.

BEA's current practice is not to capitalize investment in human capital, either by schools or corporations. Therefore, I exclude the cost of selecting and training actors from my analysis.

1a.   Nominal Revenue Data

The main data source for this paper is the 2007 Economic Census. According to the 2007 Economic Census, performing arts companies and independent artists received $13.7 billion of revenue and donations in 2007. Out of that $13.7 billion, popular music concerts earned $2.9 billion. That revenue has already been counted in a separate paper on the music industry (Soloveichik 2013a). Therefore, the Economic Census product-line receipts (collected only for establishments with payroll) from theatrical plays, operas, dances and other performance arts was $9.8 billion. After accounting for firms without payroll, which are sizable in this industry, and adjusting for misreporting and non-filers, total receipts for live performances was $13.3 billion.[1]

I use a variety of sources to estimate revenue from 1929 to 2010. The Service Annual Survey provides performing art revenue from 1998 to 2010. The Census of Services reports revenues for commercial performing arts companies in 1972, 1977, 1982, 1987 and 1992. Before 1972, I used BEA's estimates of consumer spending on live entertainment as a proxy for performing arts revenue.[2] Finally, I interpolated missing years to get the annual revenue.

Only 12% of ticket sales revenue[3] and 18% of performance contract fees are used to pay script licensing fees. Hired performers do not generally supply their own advertising, so they are able to spend a larger percentage of their revenue on original scripts. The remaining revenue is

---

[1] The BEA makes use of two studies to adjust Census values for two known deficiencies: misreporting and non-filers. The IRS National Research Program Study data is employed to adjust receipts data for underreporting. From the Bureau of Census, the Exact-Match Study estimates non-filer adjustments by making use of records from the Social Security Administration and the IRS to determine estimates of receipts from establishments that failed to file.
[2] Some sources in the literature suggest that private donations and government grants as a percentage of revenue rose from 1929 to 1965. Accordingly, consumer spending growth may underestimate total revenue growth. Since 1965, private donations and government grants have stayed fixed at about 40% of total revenues.
[3] Performing arts companies also earn money from donations, fees for providing entertainment and corporate sponsorships. I treat those revenue sources the same as ticket sales.

spent on actor salaries, props, marketing and other performance expenses. The estimate of 12% for ticket sales and 18% for performance contracts is based on rules of thumb in the industry literature (Baumol and Bowen 1966) and (Conte and Langley 2007). Based on the ticket sales and contract fees reported in the 2007 Economic Census, I calculate that 13.44% of the $13.3 billion earned by performing arts companies is used to pay script licensing fees (including implicit licensing fees earned by artists who perform their own scripts). As a robustness check, I also collected data from Broadway.org that gives average prices for individual plays. I found that ticket prices are consistently lower for non-copyrighted plays like Shakespeare than for copyrighted plays. This result shows that theatrical play scripts are an important cost for performing arts companies.

Because my paper is focused on investment in new theatrical play scripts, I would like to report revenue by year of first performance rather than current performance. In other words, a 2010 performance if "Hamlet" is attributed to the early 1600's, when Shakespeare first wrote the play. Of course, I don't know how much new scripts released in 2010 will earn in the future. I will use data on current market shares for new plays and old plays to predict future earnings. This data is described further in section 1c. Given my predicted earnings, I calculate the net present value (NPV) of new play scripts:

Nominal Investment = (Sales of New Plays)*[(NPV of all Sales)/(Sales in First Year)]

In section 1c., I calculate that new plays account for 18% of total industry sales. I also calculate that the net present value (NPV) of all future sales is 4.27 times sales in the first year (at 7% real discount rate).[4] Therefore, I calculate:

Investment = (Total Industry Sales)*.18*4.27 = 77% of Total Industry Sales.

---

[4]The 7% discount rate deflates future sales by the PCE deflator, **not** the play script price index. Over the past 20 years, wholesale script prices have grown faster than the PCE. However, I believe investors holding play scripts are concerned with revenues relative to GDP, not revenues relative to the play script industry.

Figure 1 shows the annual revenue earned by play scripts and nominal investment in new play scripts from 1929 to 2010. At first glance, it might seem strange that production is always lower than total industry sales. However, this is a natural consequence of my discount rate. Play scripts are long-lived capital assets, so many authors must wait five, ten or even fifty years before they earn money. These future revenues occur far in the future, so they are discounted heavily when valuing a new script.

1b.   Prices for Live Theater and Real Revenue

Figure 2 show the price index for live theater from 1929 to 2008. My price index is taken from BEA's personal consumption expenditures price index for live entertainment. That price index is available in NIPA table 2.4.4U, line 211. I then adjust the BEA's price deflator to account for the fact that live music concert prices rose significantly faster than the overall performing arts industry.[5] As discussed earlier, I track live music concerts when calculating investment in original music assets, and so that inflation has already been counted in a separate paper (Soloveichik 2013a). Before 1959, I use the price for Broadway tickets as a proxy for overall theater prices (Baumol and Bowen 1966).[6]

Figure 3 shows the real revenue from performance art from 1929 to 2008. Real ticket sales fell by almost 40% between 1995 and 2008. The decrease was gradual and started well before the financial crash – so it is not just consumers cutting back in the recession. The decrease may be related to the New York real estate boom, which raised costs for Broadway theaters.

---

[5] I only have data on live music concert prices and revenues back to 1984. Before then, I assume that concerts accounted for a fixed share of performing arts revenues, and they had the same inflation rate as the overall industry.
[6] They report top ticket prices only. I assume that average ticket prices grow at the same rate as top ticket prices. The book reports musical and non-musical prices separately. I average them to get overall inflation. I also smoothed across three years to minimize short-term noise.

According to an IBDB.com venue search, 15 New York City theaters were demolished and only 3 were built between 1995 and 2008. The decrease in the 2000's may also be related to Internet broadcasting, which offered alternative methods for potential playwrights to express themselves.

1c.   Depreciation Schedules for Play Scripts, Real Production and Capital Stocks

I cannot observe market prices for used entertainment originals because they are rarely sold in the open market. Instead, I will impute prices for used entertainment originals based on future revenues and sales costs. For example, suppose that a play earns X in Year 0, Y in Year 1 and Z in Year 2. Given a discount rate, ρ, the value of the play for each year is:

$$\text{Net Present Value at Release} = X + Y/(1+\rho) + Z/(1+\rho)^2$$

$$\text{Net Present Value at Year 1} = Y + Z/(1+\rho)$$

$$\text{Net Present Value at Year 2} = Z$$

My data on play revenue is taken from the website BroadwayLeague.com. That website reports the weekly ticket revenue and attendance for every major Broadway play from 1984 to 2009. I downloaded that dataset and then looked up the original writing date for each of the nearly 1,000 plays in the dataset. It is important to note that this dataset only tracks Broadway plays performed on Broadway. It is possible that those plays have a different lifespan than non-Broadway plays, dance performances, opera, etc. However, I could not find any high quality datasets for non-Broadway performances. I also could not find reliable data before 1984. For simplicity, I will assume that Broadway plays are representative of the entire performance art industry, and depreciation rates have been steady over time.

My data on sales costs for plays is taken from the industry literature. According to the one sample budget, fixed production costs such as advertising and props account for approximately 25% of total theater costs (Conte and Langley 2007 page 226). In the BroadwayLeague.com data, a little less than half of all Broadway plays are in their first year of production on Broadway.[7] Accordingly, I estimate that fixed production costs account for approximately half of total revenue in the first year after a play opens. I also estimate that variable production costs like actor salaries account for approximately half of total revenue for every year a play is produced. The remaining revenue is used to pay royalties and repay investors. All of these breakdowns are very approximate, but they are the best I could find.

Unlike most other forms of entertainment capital, advertising costs are not concentrated in the first year after release. Instead, plays are periodically revived by new directors, promote their particular production. For example, a modern adaptation of Shakespeare still requires significant upfront costs even though the play itself has not changed for centuries. Therefore, advertising costs continue to be a significant fraction of revenues for decades after a play is first written.

Figure 4 shows the depreciation schedule for scripts. Unsurprisingly, I find that early depreciation is much faster when I track revenues rather than profits. Intuitively, plays earn a lot of money in the first year of life – but that extra money is just enough to cover the initial production costs such as rehearsal time. Plays only earn profits when they've run for long enough to cover the initial costs. More surprisingly, I find that late depreciation is faster when I track profits, so the two schedules meet again about 20 years after a play is first released. This pattern can be explained by the fact that specific performances of a particular play do not last forever. Even if the play run is profitable, actors and directors prefer new challenges eventually. Accordingly, long-lived play scripts typically have several runs, each of which requires substantial upfront investments.

---

[7] Some plays opened significantly earlier in other markets, and then moved to Broadway. I assume that they needed new advertising, new sets, etc. when they moved to a larger market.

Figure 5 combines the real investment data in Figure 3 with the depreciation schedule in Figure 4 to calculate capital stocks from 1929 to 2010.[8] I also show capital schedules with a geometric depreciation rate of 11% per year. That 11% depreciation rate is the average for theatrical plays, greeting cards and stock photography. In order to simplify the calculations used to prepare the national accounts, I use that depreciation schedule to measure the capital stock of all miscellaneous artwork. This underestimates the value of theatrical plays, which are relatively long-lived. But it overestimates the value of greeting cards and stock photography. The three sub-categories will be consolidated in the national accounts, so measuring each sub-category precisely is not important as long as the total is correct.

2. Greeting Cards and Other Paper Items

As a physical product, greeting cards are used once. Therefore, it might seem improper to classify greeting cards as a long-lived capital asset. However, I am only capitalizing the original design for greeting cards – not the physical product. The overwhelming majority of greeting cards are bought for occasions such as birthdays, Christmas, Mother's Day, etc. These occasions have roughly the same cultural meaning today as they did decades ago. Therefore, many card designs can be re-used year after year without revising them significantly. For example, Hallmark is still selling a card with a picture of purple pansies that was first released in 1939 (Davis 1997). In fact, the non-durable nature of the physical greeting card helps protect the long-term value of greeting card design. Individual greeting cards cannot be re-used, so consumers need to buy new greeting cards each holiday.

---

[8] In order to get capital stock in 1929, I estimate real production back to 1900. My pre-1929 real production estimates are based on Census data and the industry literature.

2a.   Nominal Revenue Data

The main data source for this paper is the 2007 Economic Census. According to the Economic Census, greeting card publishers sold $4.5 billion worth of cards in 2007. I increase revenues by 7% to account for underreporting and misreported in the greeting card industry. My data on nominal revenue is taken from a variety of surveys conducted by the Census Department. The Service Annual Survey reports revenues for greeting card publishers between 1998 and 2010. The Economic Census reports revenues for greeting card publishers in 2002 and 1997. Finally, the Census of Manufactures reports revenues for greeting card publishers in 1931, 1933, 1935, 1937, 1939, 1947, 1950-1954, 1958, 1963-1972, 1977 and 1982-1992. Finally, I interpolate the missing years to get the annual revenue from greeting card sales for every year from 1929 to 2007.

I assume that 15% of the revenue from greeting cards is a return on the original design. Most of the revenue goes to pay manufacturing costs such as printing, sales costs such as delivery to stores, etc. In the book 'Art Marketing 101', Constance Smith (1998) estimates that approximately 10% of the wholesale price for a card should be attributed to the artwork itself, 55% for production and sales costs and 35% for profit and overhead. Allocating the overhead and profit proportionally, I calculate that 15% of the wholesale revenue from greeting card sales should be attributed to the original design. Another book, 'Publishing Your Art as Cards, Posters and Calendars' (Davis 1997) gives a similar breakdown.[9] In the remainder of the paper, I will assume that this 15% allocation has been constant from 1929 to 2010.[10]

---

[9] Both of these books are written for small artists who are considering producing greeting cards. I talked with an employee at a major greeting card company. She said that her company had roughly similar costs to the industry literature, but would not give exact figures.

[10] The Census of Manufactures reports the ratio of value of materials to value of inputs) for a selected sample of years. This ratio has steadily decreased from around 40% in 1958 to only 18% in 1992. It is possible that the sales costs for greeting cards have increased to compensate for the decreased material costs. If the sales costs have not

Figure 6 shows greeting card investment from 1929 to 2010. Just like theatrical play scripts, I adjust the revenue numbers to account for a lag between production and sales. I have not been able to find any data to measure the ratio of investment to revenue for greeting cards. In the absence of data, I assume that greeting cards are similar to book. In a separate paper on books, I estimated that new book investment is 79% of current revenue (Soloveichik 2013b)

2b.   Prices for Greeting Cards and Real Sales

Figure 7 shows a price index for greeting cards from 1929 to 2010. My price data is taken from a variety of government and industry sources. Between 1986 and 2010, the BLS publishes a producer price index (PPI) for greeting card publishers. I used that PPI without any changes. Between 1982 and 1986, I used the BLS PPI for periodical publishers. Between 1954 and 1982, I used data from the Census of Manufactures to create a rough price index. For selected years, the Census of Manufactures asks both the number of greeting cards printed and total earnings. I then used those numbers to calculate the average wholesale price for a greeting card. Between 1929 and 1954, I could not find any reliable data on greeting card prices. I will use book price indexes as a proxy for greeting card prices (Soloveichik 2013b). Finally, I spliced all four price series together to get a single price index for greeting cards from 1929 to 2012.

Figure 8 shows real revenue from greeting card designs. I first combine the nominal sales data in Figure 6 with the price index in Figures 7 to calculate real sales. I then multiply the real sales by 15% to get the real revenue from greeting card designs from 1929 to 2007. The most striking result from Figure 8 is that real greeting card revenues declined by 28% from 1998 to 2007. This decline is consistent with a general decline in personal letters. Between 1998 and 2007, real consumer expenditures on postage fell by 33%. Instead, people are choosing to write

---

increased, then the percent of revenues devoted to artwork has risen over time. In that case, Figure 6 underestimates the real growth in the greeting card industry.

e-mails. It is also possible that some customers are using home computers to design and print cards themselves. Unlike commercial card designs, these home-made designs are considered outside the scope of GDP. Therefore, they are not counted in capital stock. [11]

2c.   Depreciation Schedules, Real Production and Capital Stocks

I was not able to estimate the depreciation schedule for greeting card designs. Based on the industry literature and conversations with industry experts, I am confident that many greeting card designs survive for decades after they are first published. As a result, greeting card designs are definitely a long-lived capital asset. However, no industry source could give me a specific depreciation rate. I was also unable to find any datasets that track individual greeting card sales over time. For example, the Nielsen Bookscan data reports some greeting cards sales – but they do not separate individual designs. Because I could not find any greeting card sales data, I take my depreciation rate from my paper on the book industry (Figure 10) (Soloveichik 2013b).

Figure 9 combines the real investment data in Figure 8 and the depreciation schedule for books to calculate greeting card design stocks from 1929 to 2010.[12] I also show capital schedules with a geometric depreciation rate of 11% per year. That 11% depreciation rate is the average for theatrical plays, greeting cards and stock photography. This depreciation rate overestimates the greeting card stock, which partially balances the underestimate in Figure 5.

---

[11] Many consumers purchase prepackaged software to help them design cards. That prepackaged software is generally a copy of software originals owned by greeting card publishers or other software designers. BEA already capitalizes the software original in the NIPAs.
[12] In order to get capital stock in 1929, I estimate real production back to 1900. My pre-1929 real production estimates are based on Census data and the industry literature.

3. Commercial Photography

In 2007, commercial photographers earned $2.7 billion from the sale and licensing of their photographs. The main customers for commercial photographs are advertisers. For example, a supermarket might need a beautiful picture of apples to illustrate their weekly sales flyer. In addition, magazine and newspaper publishers often license pre-existing commercial pictures to illustrate a story. For example, a story on a new cholesterol drug might include a picture of the heart to set the general tone. Finally, a wide variety of industries occasionally license photographs to add color to their important memos, jazz up boxes, etc.

Because commercial photography is mainly used by advertisers and magazine publishers, it might seem that commercial photography cannot count as an entertainment original. After all, BEA's official policy is to treat all advertising expenditures as an intermediate expense, and not an investment activity. Similarly, the OECD handbook recommends that magazine and newspaper production be treated as an intermediate expense rather than an investment activity (OECD 2010 33.5). Only a small fraction of commercial photography is licensed by industries producing long-lived entertainment assets such as book publishers, recording studios etc.

In fact, commercial photography is an entirely separate product than advertising, magazine publishing or newspaper publishing. The typical commercial picture is produced by a photographer working by him or herself. The photographer might hire models and arrange a very specific picture, or they might just snap a picture that came naturally. The photographer then posts the picture on a stock photography service like Getty Images.[13] Months or even years later, an advertiser searches on Getty Images and decides to license that pre-existing picture for a

---

[13] Many stock photography services also sell some images on their own websites or through other channels.

particular ad campaign. In most cases, the license only covers use in a particular ad campaign – photographers are still free to license their picture to other advertisers.[14] Throughout the picture's entire lifecycle, the original photographer keeps the copyright. Advertisers use pictures to produce their final product in the same way they use other capital assets like computer software, songs, and cars.

A second potential objection to counting photography as a capital asset is that some pictures have a very short lifespan for their photographers. For example, a wedding photographer makes virtually all of his or her money by selling albums to the family shortly after the wedding. Similarly, a picture showing a particular current event is only useful for the few days that stories are still being written about that event. However, these types of pictures are already excluded from the commercial photography industry that I am studying. Personal photography services like wedding photographs are tracked separately from commercial photography in the Service Annual Survey, Economic Census and Census of Services. And newspapers typically employ their own photographers for current events, and so those costs are included in the newspaper industry. The main pictures tracked in my category 'commercial photography' are long-lived pictures licensed to advertisers, magazine publishers and newspaper publishers. Later in this section, I will show that these pictures have a useful lifespan of much longer than 1 year. Accordingly, it is entirely reasonable to treat commercial photographs, and only commercial photographs, as a capital asset.

---

[14] The licensing agreement may prohibit future advertisers whose products incompatible with the first advertiser's niche. For example, Disney might not want a picture it uses to appear later in a cigarette commercial. The licensing fee is generally higher when there are more restrictions on re-use.

3a.   Nominal Revenue Data

In the 2007 Economic Census, commercial photographers report $1.6 billion of revenue. BEA adjusts that reported revenue upwards by 73% to account for underreporting and mis-reporting in the Economic Census. Therefore, total revenue for commercial photographers is $2.7 billion. My historical data is taken from a variety of sources. The Service Annual Survey reports revenues for commercial photographers 1998 and 2010. The Economic Census reports revenues for commercial photographers in 2002 and 1997. The Census of Services reports revenues for commercial photographers in 1972, 1977, 1982, 1987 and 1992. Before 1972, I could not find any data specific to commercial photography. Instead, I used the occupational and income data in the population Census to estimate the total earnings for all photographers, regardless of industry, from 1920 to 1980. I use that revenue as a proxy for commercial photography revenue.[15] Finally, I interpolate between my data points to get annual revenue from commercial photography from 1929 to 2010.

Once a photographer has shot a picture, he or she has two main methods to earn money from that picture: 1) Contracting with a stock photo agency to sell the picture for him; or 2) Selling it by himself or herself. Stock photo agencies generally charge a commission of about 50% of the gross licensing fee (Heron and MacTavish 1997). I was not able to find any specific estimate of the sales costs when a photographer sells his work himself, so I assume 50% sales costs.

Even if sales costs are always 50% of photo licensing fees, it is still extremely difficult to determine the average sales costs relative to reported revenue. Photographers who license their photos through stock agencies never see the 50% kept by the stock agency. Accordingly, I will assume that they report only the money they keep to the Service Annual Survey. This licensing

---

[15] (Commercial Photography Revenues)/(Photographer Earnings in the Census) fell steadily from 1972 to 2007. If the same trend occurred before 1972, then my index slightly under-estimated commercial photography production before 1972. In practice, I estimate that real production of commercial photographs was very low before 1972, so a large percentage error has a small effect on overall entertainment production.

fee is a pure return on their entertainment capital, without any sales costs. On the other hand, a photographer who sells his work himself pays about 50% of his revenue for marketing costs. Accordingly, the formula for sales costs is:

Sales Costs = (Total Revenue)*50%*[1-(Market Share for Stock Agencies)]

In my review of the industry literature, I was unable to find any time series data on the market share for stock agencies. For simplicity, I will assume that stock agencies always represent 50% of the market. Accordingly, sales costs are always 25% of revenue.

Figure 10 shows nominal investment and nominal revenue from stock photography from 1929 to 2010. Just like theatrical movies and greeting card designs, I adjust the nominal revenue data to account for the lag between release and sale. This adjustment is based on a depreciation schedule that will be described in more detail in section 3c. On average, I calculate that new investment equals 60% of existing revenue.

3b.   Prices for Stock Photography and Real Sales

Figure 11 shows my price index for stock photography. That price index for stock photography is taken from BEA's pre-existing index for photo studios. That price index is given in NIPA Table 2.4.4U, line 217. Before then, I use Census data on photographer wages to construct a price index. It is possible that the price index given in Figure 11 overestimates inflation in the past decade. There are now online resources where anybody can search for and license digital pictures for a couple of dollars. A high volume user can also buy a CD containing thousands of pictures for less than $50. However, I have not been able to locate any consumer price data for stock photography. Furthermore, the biggest price drops happened for casual users, who use very little stock photography. Big users like advertising firms and magazines are less likely to benefit from stock photo websites. Figure 12 shows real investment back to 1929.

15

3c.   Depreciation Rates for Stock Photography.

I use data from the website Istockphoto.com to get the depreciation schedule for stock photography. Istockphoto gives each photo a unique identification number and reports when that picture was first uploaded to the website. In addition, Istockphoto reports how many times each picture on their website was downloaded.[16] In order to estimate the depreciation schedule, I created a list of all photos on the website with more than 50 downloads in August 2009 and February 2010.[17] I then calculated the download rate by age.[18] I do not have any data on sales costs by age. I will assume that sales costs are proportional to gross revenue. Therefore, I can discount gross revenues to get the NPV of a picture at any point in time.

Figure 13 shows the depreciation schedule for commercial stock photography. On average, photos depreciate by about 20% per year. The depreciation rate is slightly faster for new photos and slower for old photos. This is reasonably consistent with the industry literature. In their 2006 10-k filing, Getty Images used a four-year lifespan to depreciate their contemporary photographs and a fifty-year lifespan for historical photos. Similarly, the book "The Real Business of Photography" (Weisgrau 2004) suggests a three to five year lifespan.

Figure 14 shows capital stock of commercial photos from 1929 to 2010. These numbers are calculated from the depreciation schedule in Figure 13 and the real investment numbers in Figure 12. Just like theatrical movies and greeting cards, I also show the capital stock with an 11% depreciation rate. That rate will be used for the broader category "miscellaneous artwork". Adding up all the sub-categorie, the 11% geometrical rate produces similar estimates for

---

[16] Istockphoto charges higher prices for versions with more pixels, so downloads does not match sales precisely.
[17] I truncated the list at 50 to simplify the task of collecting the data. My estimated depreciation rate decreases when I use a higher truncation point. I do not know what depreciation rates would be if I included all photos.
[18] In practice, I looked at relative download rate, which controls for quality changes in photos over time. I assume that all photos were uploaded shortly after creation. It is possible that some photos were uploaded later.

aggregate capital stock as calculating capital stock for each sub-category individually based on their own depreciation rate.

Conclusion

This paper measured nominal investment, prices and capital stock for three small categories of entertainment. The national accounts, all three types will be combined into a single line item: miscellaneous artwork. In 2007, I estimate that total investment in miscellaneous artwork was $3.3 billion. By category, theatrical play scripts were $1.4 billion, greeting card designs were $0.5 billion and commercial stock photography was $1.4 billion. Taken individually, each of the entertainment categories described earlier are too small to examine in a single paper. Therefore, I will combine all three small categories into a single paper.

To review, my main empirical results were:

1) Miscellaneous artwork has grown slower than the overall entertainment sector;

2) Miscellaneous artwork has a long useful lifespan, with an average depreciation rate of 11% per year. The capital value of all miscellaneous artwork was $32 billion in 2010 (2005 dollars).

Figure 1: Nominal Investment from 1929 to 2010

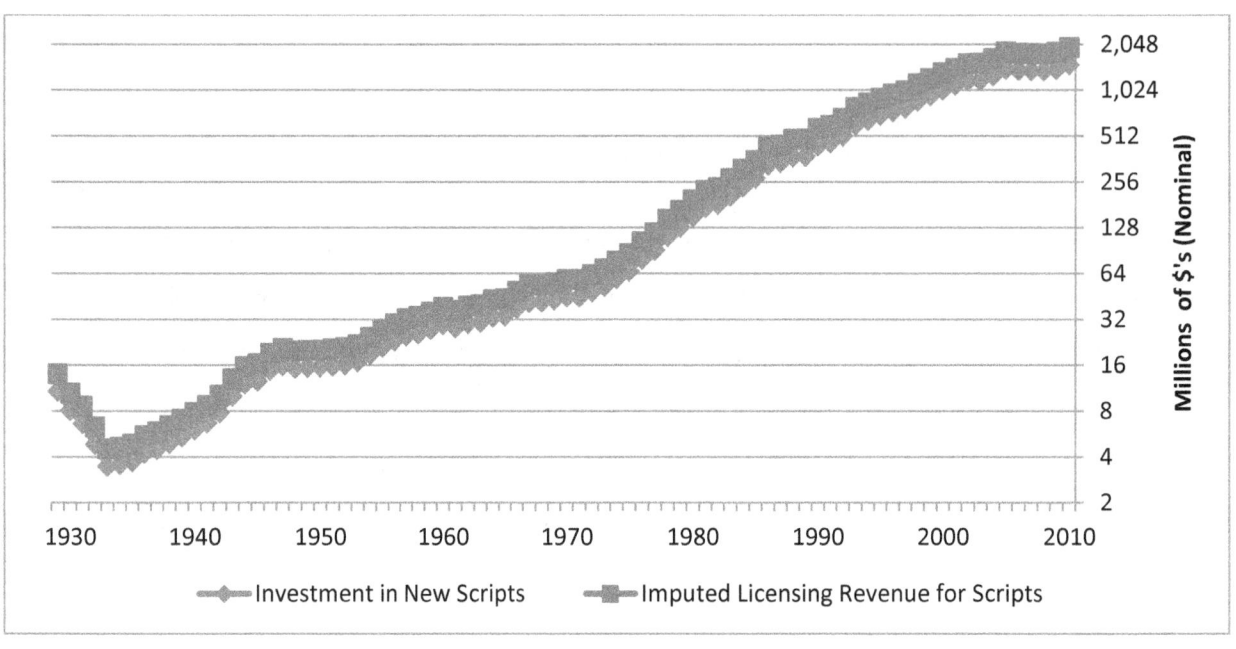

Figure 2: Price Index for Play Scripts, 1929 to 2010

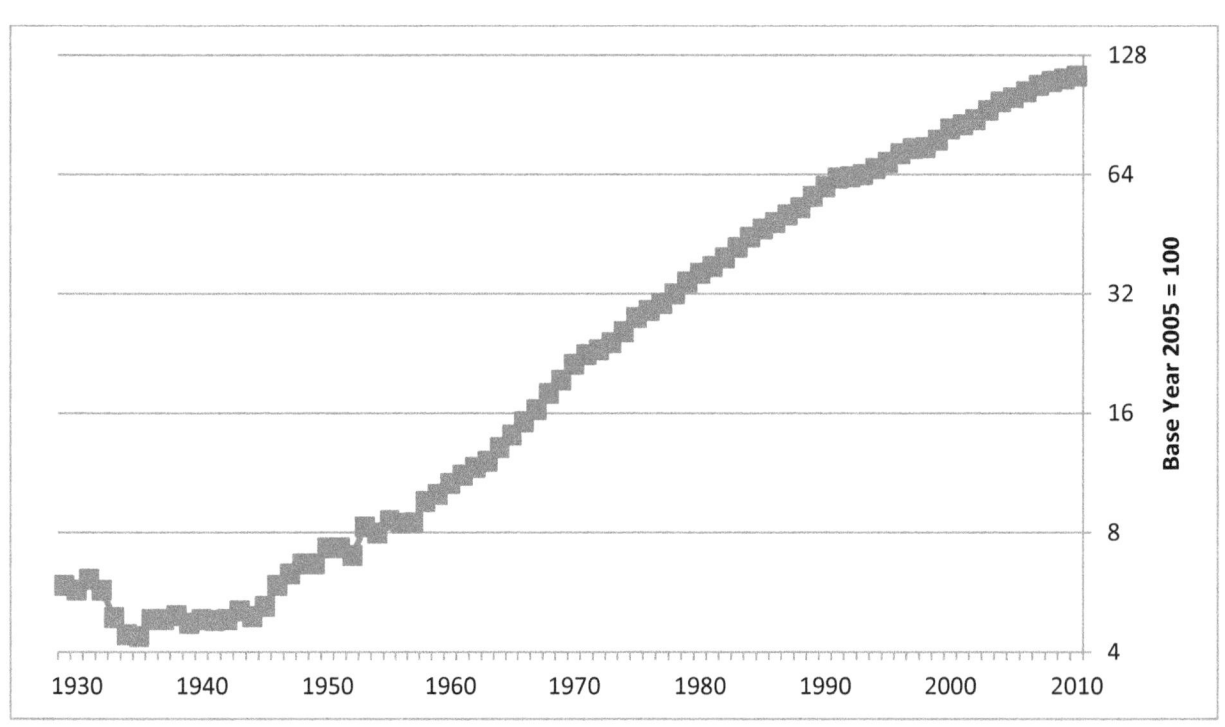

Figure 3: Real Investment from 1929 to 2010

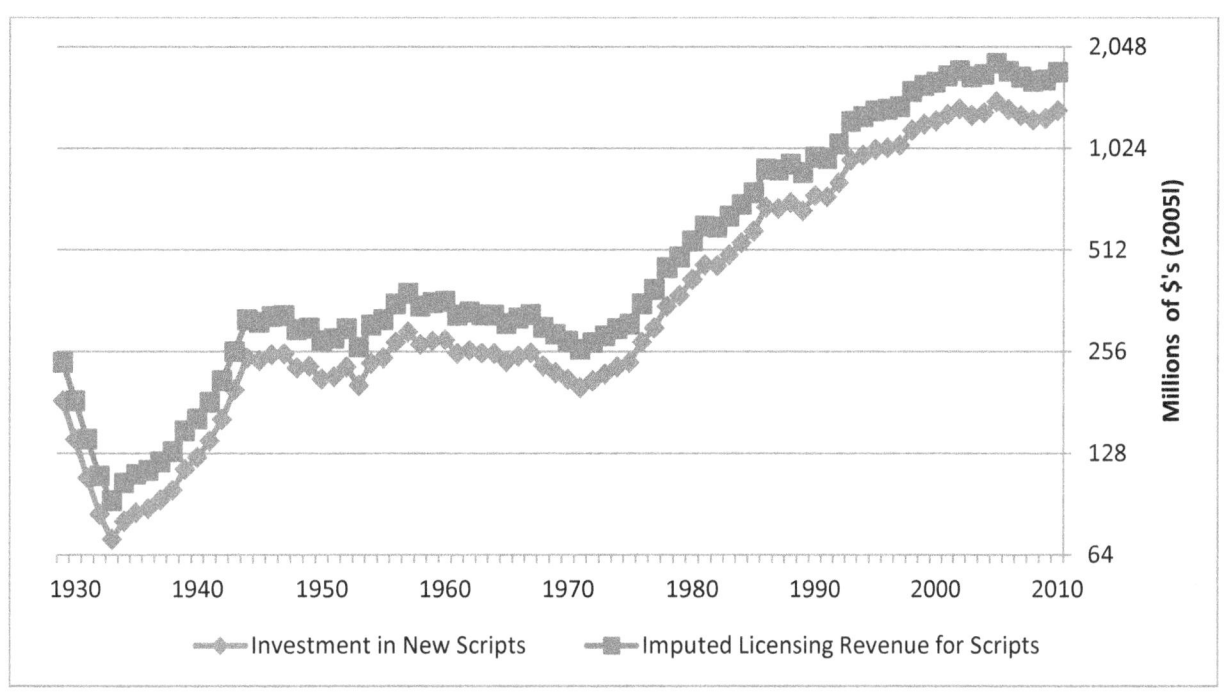

Figure 4: Depreciation Schedule for Play Scripts

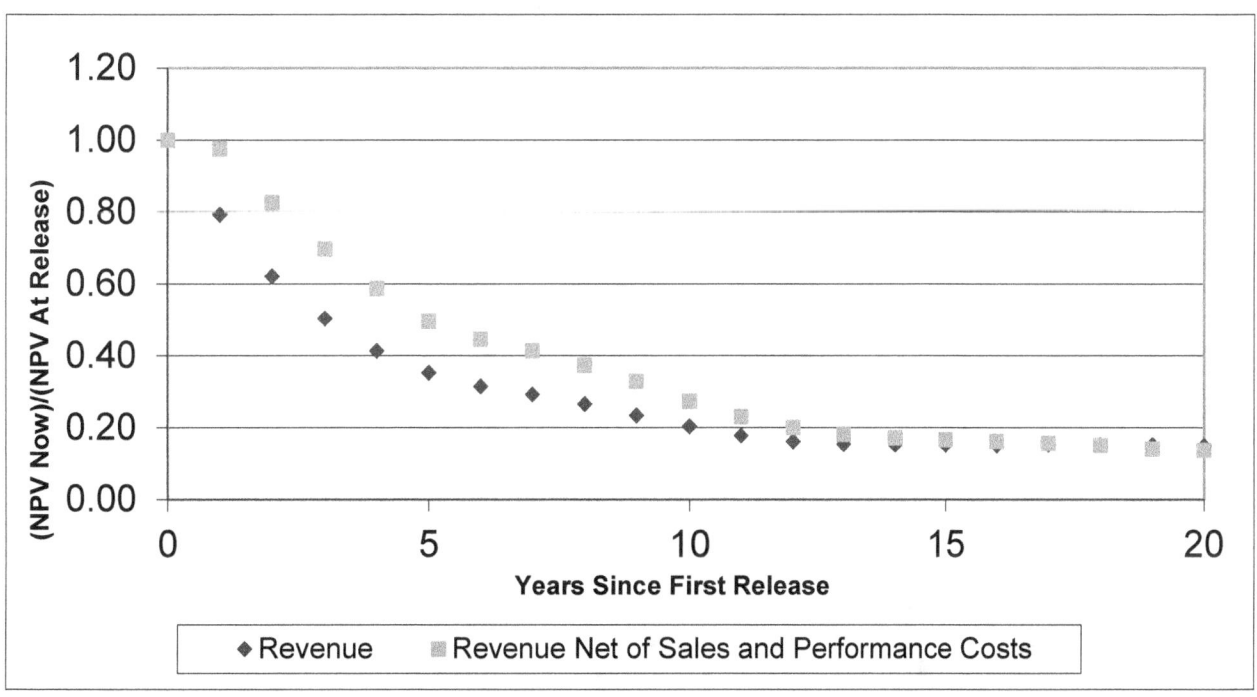

Figure 5: Capital Stock of Play Scripts, 1929-2010

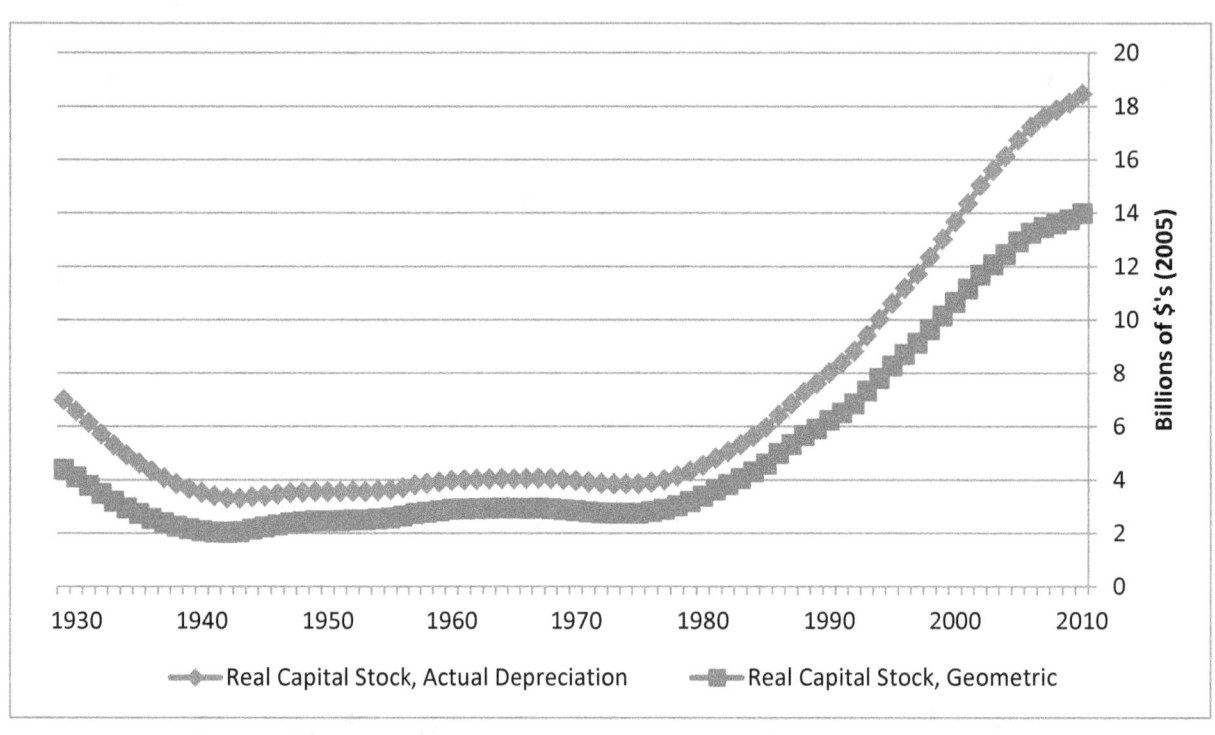

Figure 6: Nominal Investment in Greeting Card Designs

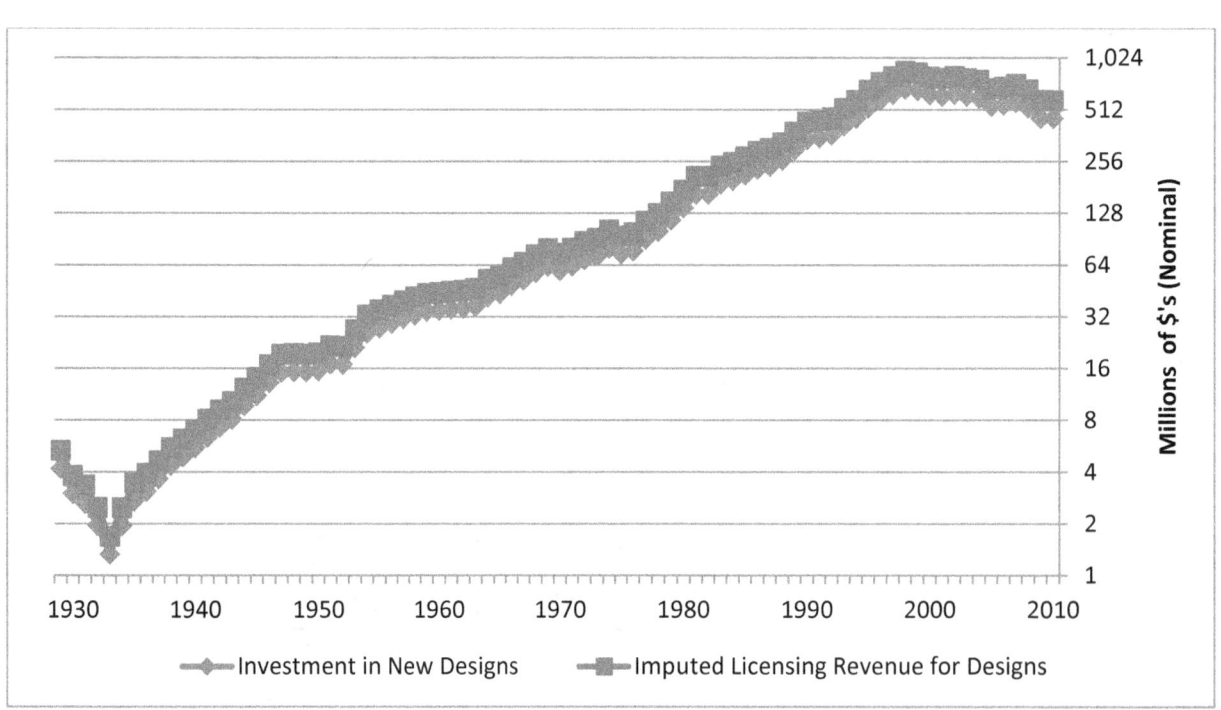

Figure 7: Price Indexes for Greeting Card Designs

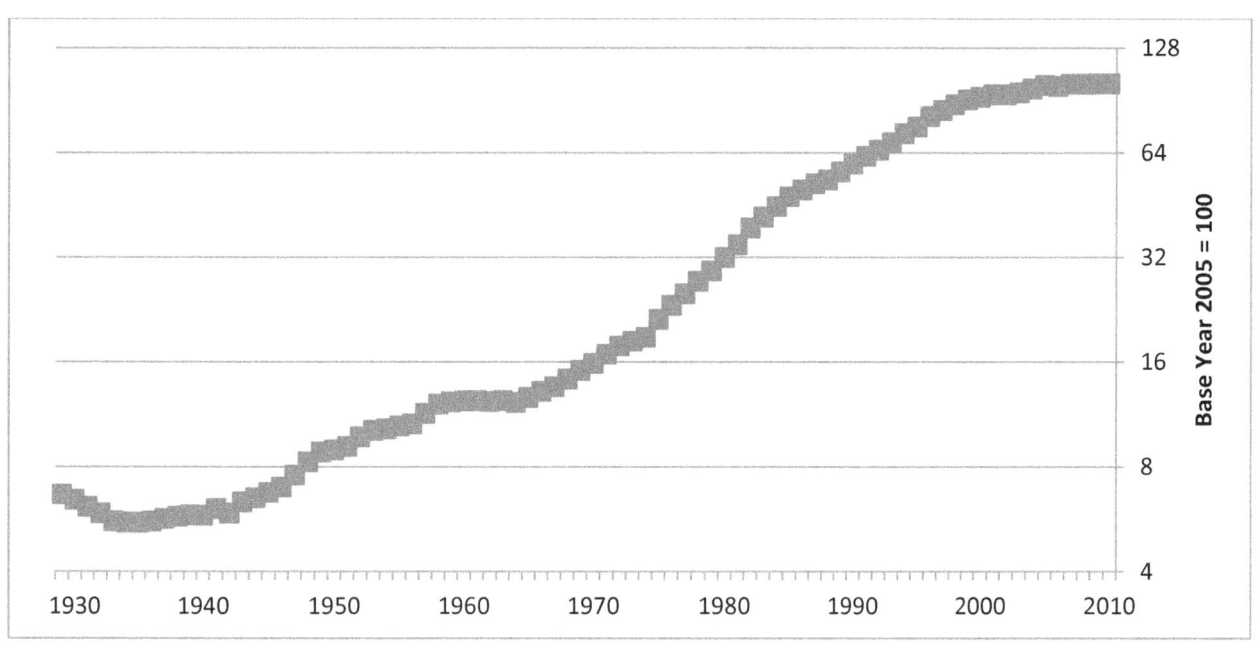

Figure 8: Real Investment for Greeting Card Designs

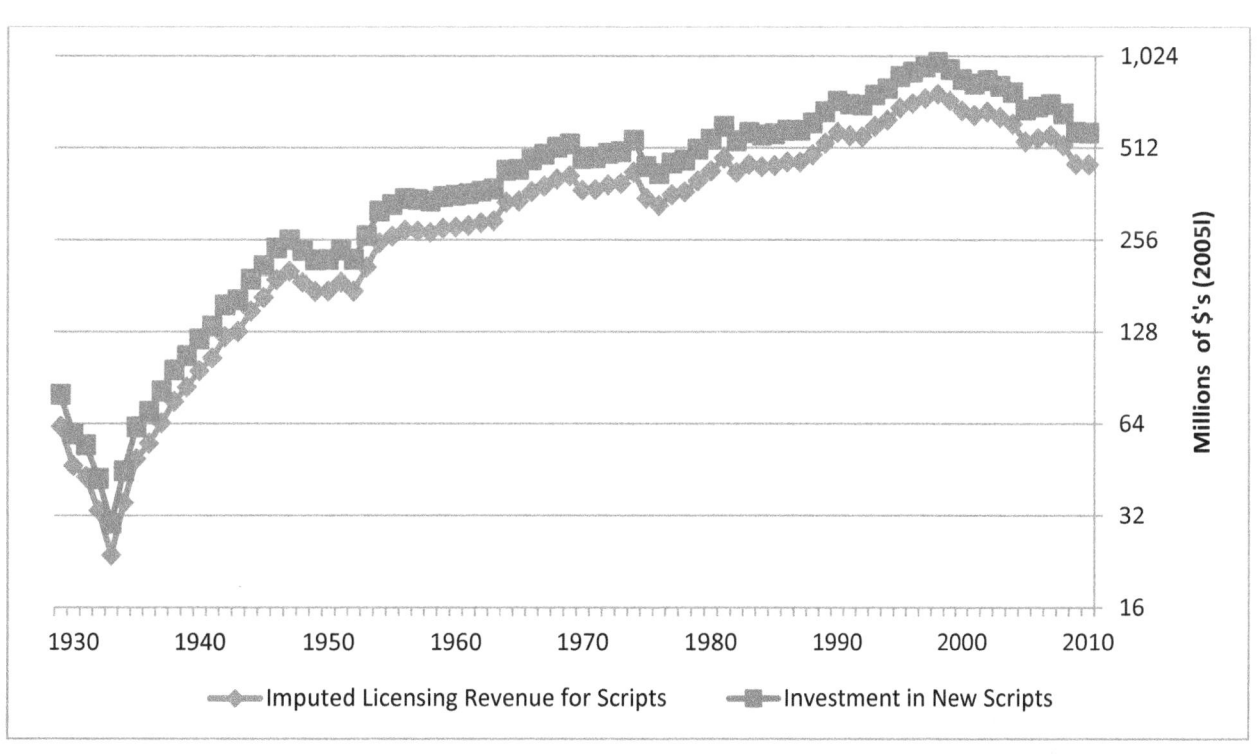

Figure 9: Capital Stock of Greeting Card Designs

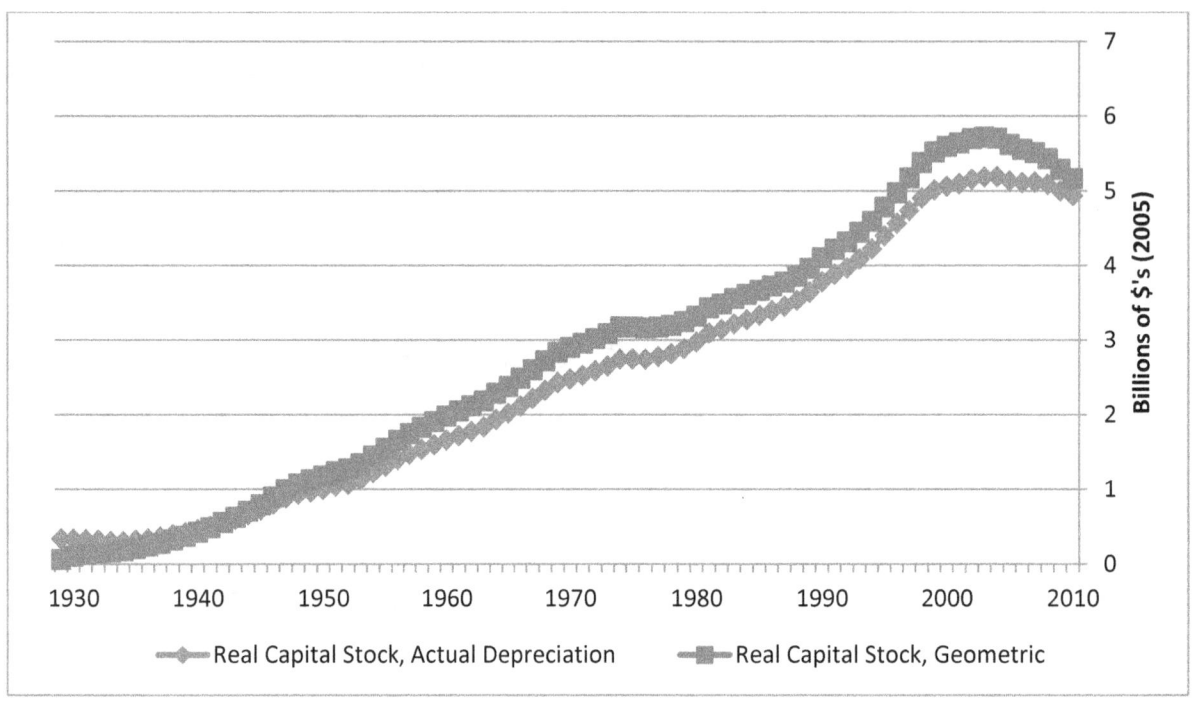

Figure 10: Nominal Investment in Stock Photography

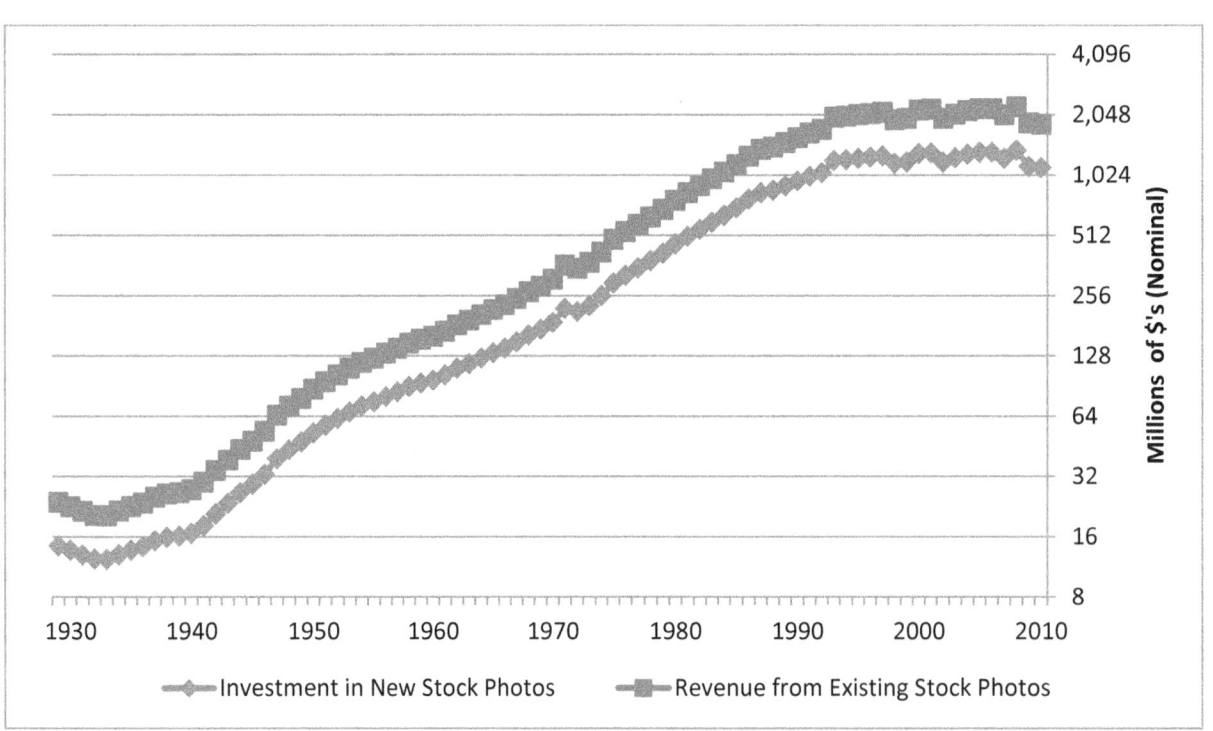

Figure 11: Price Indexes for Stock Photography

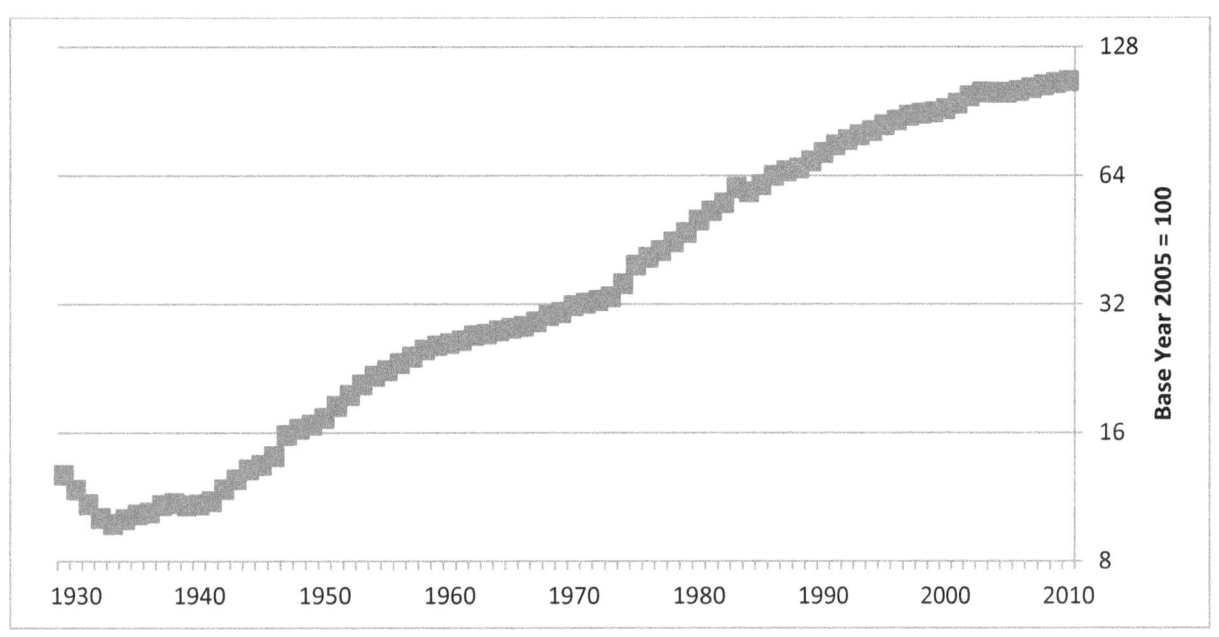

Figure 12: Real Investment In Stock Photography

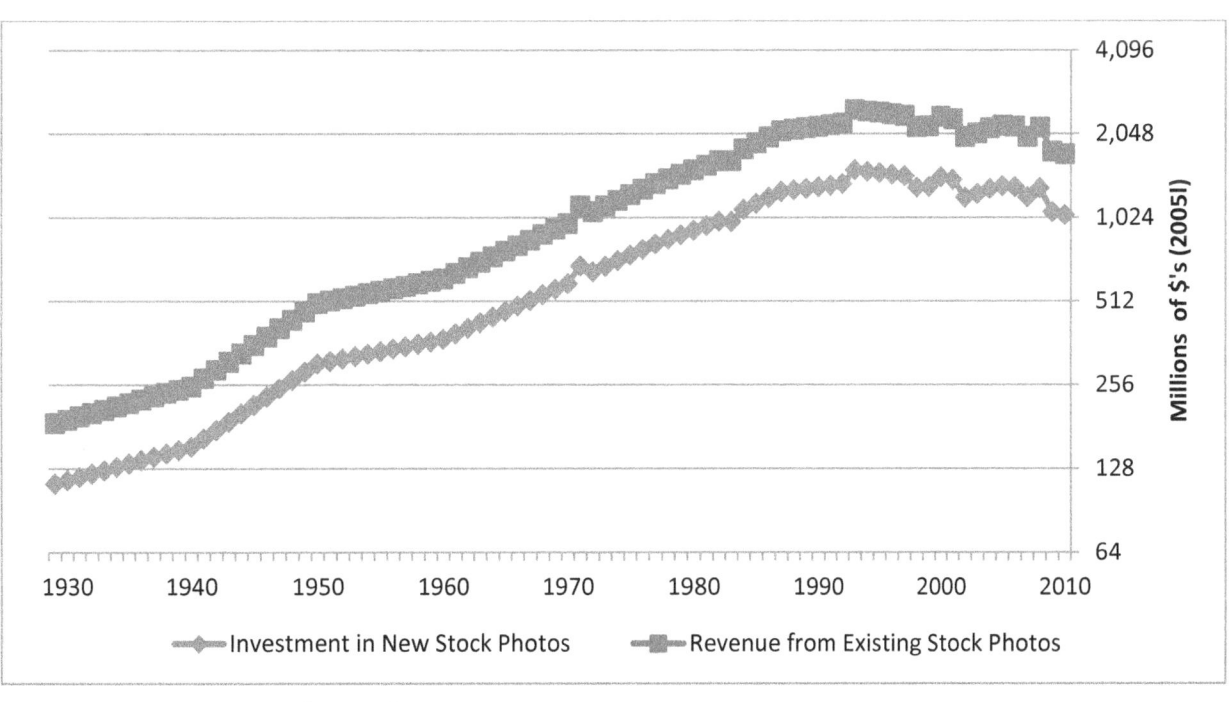

Figure 13: Depreciation Rates for Stock Photography

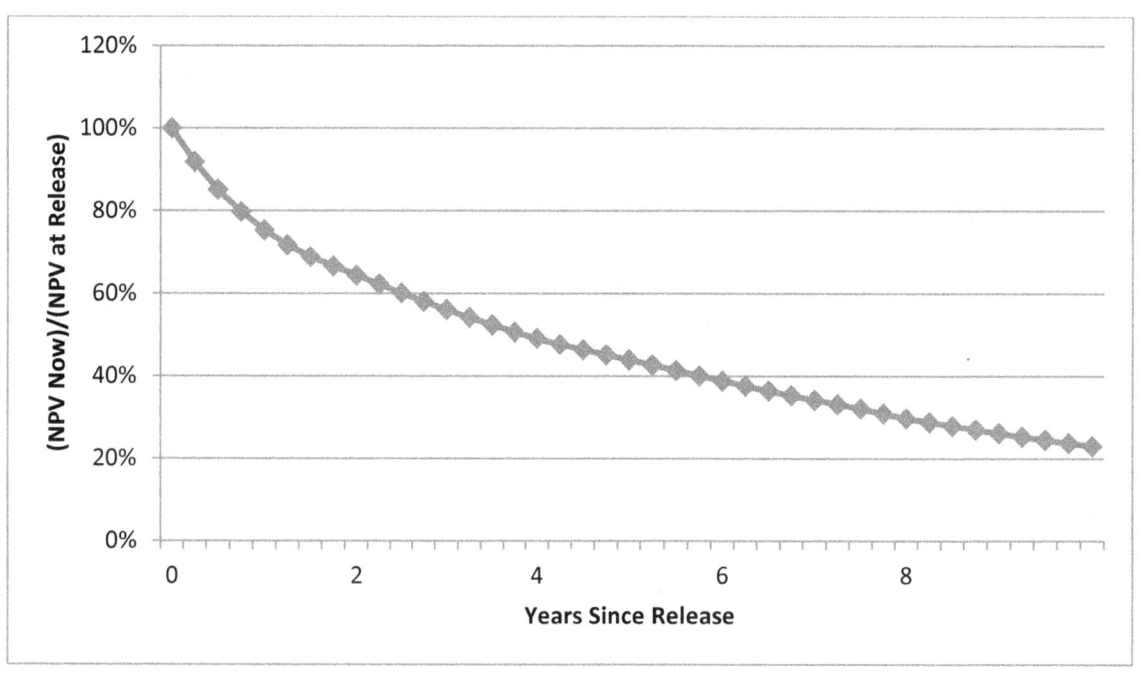

Figure 14: Capital Values for Stock Photography

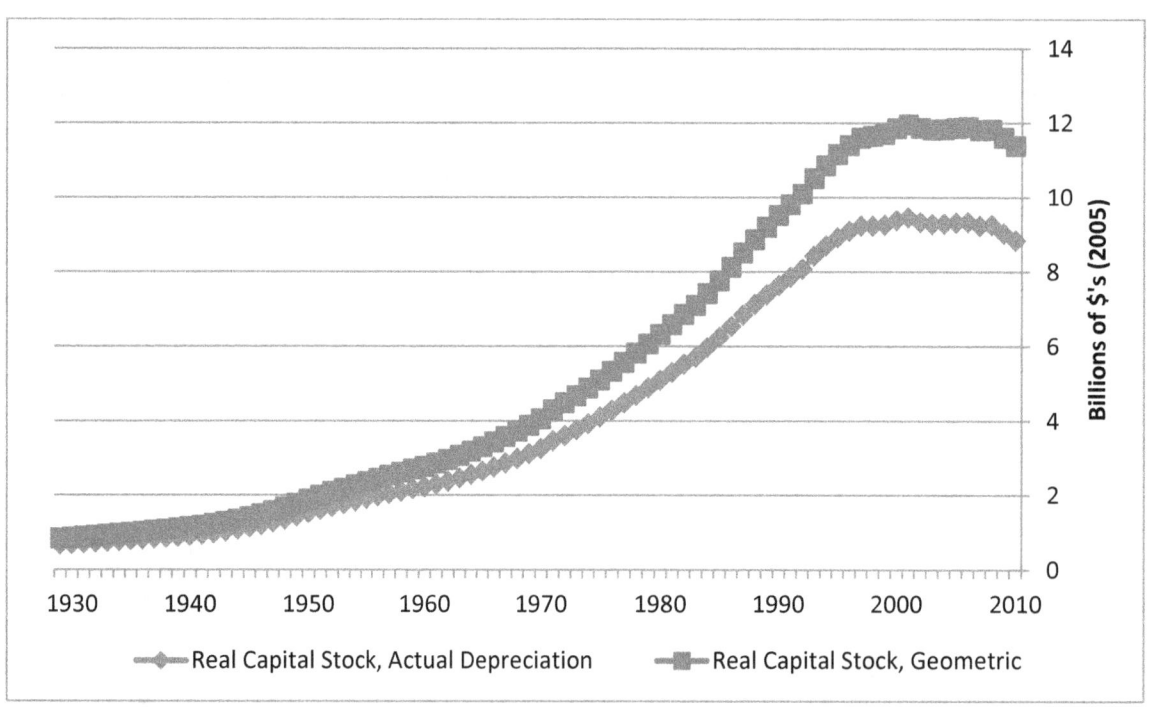

Bibliography

Bakker, Gerben. (2010). Productivity growth in personal services from lagging to leading: how motion pictures industrialized entertainment. Manuscript

Baumol, William and Bowen, William. (1966). *Performing Arts, the Economic Dilemma* Twentieth Century Fund. MIT Press

Conte, David and Langley, Stephen. (2007). *Theater Management, Producing and Managing the Performing Arts.* Entertainment Pro

Davis, Harold. (1997). *Publishing Your Art As Card, Posters & Calendars* Consultant Press

Farber, Donald. (1997). *Production Theater, Second Revised Edition.* Proscenium Publishers.

Heron, Michal and MacTavish, David. (1997) *Pricing Photographer, the Complete Guide to Assignment & Stock Prices* Allsworth Press

Poggi, Jack. (1968). *Theater in America, The Impact of Economic Forces 1870-1967.* Cornell University Press

OECD. (2010). Handbook on Deriving Capital Measures for Intellectual Property Production. www.oecd.org/std/na/44312350.pdf

Smith, Constance. (1998). *Art Marketing 101.* Published by Artnetwork

Soloveichik, Rachel. (2013a). Music Originals As Capital Assets. manuscript

Soloveichik, Rachel. (2013b). Books As Capital Assets. manuscript

Soloveichik, Rachel. (2013c). Long-Lived Television Programs As Capital Assets. manuscript

Soloveichik, Rachel. (2013d). Theatrical Movies as Capital Assets. Manuscript

United Nations Statistics Division. (2008). Updated System of National Accounts 2008. Accessed May 20 2013. http://unstats.un.org/unsd/nationalaccount/sna2008.asp

Weisgrau, Richard. (2004). *The Real Business of Photography.* Allsworth Press